T2-AJT-240*

D0568036

THE SIOUX

by Barbara Brooks

Illustrated by Luciano Lazzarino

ROURKE PUBLICATIONS, INC.

VERO BEACH, FLORIDA 32964

LIBRARY
California School for the Deaf
Riverside

CONTENTS

© 1989 by Rourke Publications, Inc.

All rights reserved. No part of this book may be reproduced or utilized in any form or by any means, electronic or mechanical including photocopying, recording, or by any information storage and retrieval system without permission in writing from the publisher.

Library of Congress Cataloging-in-Publication Data

Brooks, Barbara, 1946-
  The Sioux / by Barbara Brooks.
    p. cm. —(Native American people)
  Includes index.
  Summary: Examines the history, traditional lifestyle, and current situation of the Sioux, or Dakota, Indians, with an emphasis on the Teton Sioux group.
  1. Dakota Indians—Juvenile literature. 2. Teton Indians—Juvenile literature. [1. Teton Indians. 2. Dakota Indians 3. Indians of North America.] I. Title. II. Series.
E99.D1B85 1989 973'.0497—dc19   88-25001
        ISBN 0-86625-382-3   AC

973
BRD
11.95
1/95
Pub. — replacement

INTRODUCTION

Early in their history the Siouan group of tribes ranged from Florida to Virginia and the Carolinas. They were descendants of the groups of people thought to have migrated from Asia to North America across an ice bridge. Straight black hair and other features seemed to relate them to the Chinese and Japanese. Columbus called the first true native Americans "Indians" because he thought he was in India.

The Siouan people occupied more territory than any other group of Indians. A restless people, they started on their great migrations around 1500. Some groups moved northwest. Others traveled westward across the wilderness until they reached the Pacific.

Some of these people settled in Minnesota. They called themselves Dakotas, meaning "allies" or "friends." The Ojibwe (Chippewa) Indians, who were often at war with the Dakotas, named them "nadowe-is-iw." This meant "adder" or "snake." French explorers shortened the Ojibwe word to "Sioux," the name commonly used today.

The three major divisions of the Sioux nation migrated to the Great Plains at different times. The largest division was and still is the Western or Teton Sioux. They were the first group to leave Minnesota and become warriors and buffalo hunters. The Teton Sioux were a colorful people and a subject of many tales. This group mounted fierce resistance to the white man's invasion of their territory. Most of the Sioux population of North and South Dakota descends from the Teton division. Today many live in South Dakota.

At the end of the seventeenth century, the middle Sioux division moved west. They split into the Yankton and Yanktonai groups. Their descendants live on reservations in North and South Dakota and in Montana.

The Eastern Sioux, also known as the Santee Sioux, were the last division to leave their Minnesota homeland. Large villages with permanent well-built bark houses were trademarks of their culture. After the Minnesota Sioux Uprising in 1862, the tribe was widely scattered. Their descendants live in North and South Dakota, Nebraska, Montana, and on small reservations in Minnesota.

3

Alaska

1st migrants
across ice·land·bridge
from Asia

Canada

the Sioux

North
Dakota
Minnesota
South Plains
Dakota   Territory
N.W. Migration
of 1500's

Westward Migration of 1500's

U.S.A.

Earliest
Virginia Settlements
N. & S. Carolina
to Florida

The Sioux Nation about the Time of Columbus

THE SIOUX nation living in the Thousand Lakes region of Minnesota were known as the Oceti Sakowin, or Seven Council Fires. Each council fire represented a different tribe. The largest tribe was the Teton. The entire Sioux nation tried to meet each summer to hold council and celebrate together with a Sun Dance. People gathered in a great camp to renew friendships. Families shared news and traded things they had gotten from other tribes.

The Sun Dance was a time for ultimate spiritual expression and celebration. At the dance, the people expressed their thanks for the past year and asked for help in the future.

The council consisted of forty-four elected chiefs. They decided future plans and the nation's policy. Four men chosen from the forty-four served as a higher authority. This was a position of great honor, respect, and dignity. Policy was suggested at this time, but each tribe functioned independently throughout the year.

Bravery, fortitude, generosity, and wisdom were four qualities all Sioux were expected to work at achieving. Chiefs were elected with these qualities in mind. Since chieftainships were not inherited, any young man who showed leadership skills could hope to become a chief. Sometimes an outstanding son of a chief was elected to succeed his father or grandfather.

Life of the Minnesota Sioux about 1600

The Sioux Indians living in Minnesota during the 1600s used the environment to their advantage. Food, shelter, tools, and other necessities came directly from the land around them. At this time, they were a woodland people living in bark lodges. The men tracked deer and small game in the forest and caught fish in the streams and lakes. The women worked in canoes gathering wild rice. Maple trees were tapped for sugar. Dogs were used to pull sleds and carry bundles. If supplies ran low in one area, they moved to another. Having lots of land and being able to travel to other places for whatever they needed was a necessity.

During their travels, the Sioux hunters occasionally managed to capture a buffalo. At this time, buffalo ranged as far east as the Appalachian mountains and were hunted on foot. Often a hunter would wear a buffalo skin to disguise his own scent and sneak close to the herd with his bow and arrow. Another tactic was to stampede a herd to a steep cliff where many buffalo would fall to their death. The Sioux realized the value of the buffalo in providing for almost all their needs: food, shelter, and clothing.

The Sioux were surrounded by tribes of superior strength. Cree Indians, and other tribes who were old enemies of the Sioux, were being supplied with firearms by French explorers. It is thought that the migration of the Sioux was due to the threat of enemy tribes with firearms and the lure of the great buffalo herds. Later the invasion of the white settlers was a factor.

In the short span of about fifty years, the first group of Sioux to migrate to the Great Plains made a transition from a woodland hunting and gathering society to a nomadic buffalo hunting society. They waged a long and bitter war with other Indian tribes living in the coveted buffalo country. Driving their enemies from this territory, the Teton Sioux were well established on the Great Plains by 1700.

(Photo courtesy of South Dakota State Historical Society)

Indians used every part of the buffalo. Here meat is drying on a scaffold.

Nomadic Life on the Plains

The life of the Sioux Indians living on the plains depended completely on the buffalo. They followed the herds and hunted the buffalo wherever possible. From the buffalo carcass came food, shelter, and clothing.

The Sioux lived in tipis, (tee PEES) which were good shelters for people on the move. Tipis were shaped like a funnel. Made from buffalo hides and poles, they were easy to move about. There was a flap on top where smoke could escape. The tipi stayed warm in the winter and cool in the summer.

The women were in charge of packing and moving the tipi. Several women working together could set up or take down a tipi in minutes. The poles from the tipi were used for a travois (trav WAH) pulled by dogs. The travois was a kind of sled where poles were attached on either side of the animal's shoulders. The other end of the poles dragged on the ground. The rest of the tipi and household goods were tied on the poles in such a fashion that old or sick people and children could ride on top of the bundle.

Prior to the advent of the horse, the only working animal the Sioux had was the dog. The dog played an important role for the Sioux in their migration onto the plains. Every family had dogs. They were tolerated but not loved by adults. A large breed about the size of a husky was preferred for working. These dogs pulled travois and carried heavy loads. A smaller type was kept for food. Dogs also served as protection and were trained to bark at strange noises.

The location of the camps was determined by the buffalo herds. Sometimes a camp might stay at a certain location for weeks or even months if meat was plentiful. The Sioux were never tied to a fixed spot. They did not grow vegetables and rarely put up permanent structures. Occasionally some families built wigwams. This type of shelter was similar to the bark houses used in Minnesota. Built during the spring rains, the wigwam protected tipi covers from rotting. It was also used to store food such as seeds, dried fruits, and vegetables that had been gathered. When this food was needed, the owner would return to claim it. Usually the Sioux tried to set up camp near water and wooded areas. Trees provided firewood and protection. They had special places to camp next to favorite rivers.

Tribal life was based on the ability to move quickly and efficiently. Their daily household goods reflected easy mobility. Everything the Sioux had could be carried by a person, dog, or later, a horse. Food and clothing were stored in soft leather bags. Cradles were adapted for easy transport. The Sioux did not make pottery, probably because it would break with all the moving.

Skins and other animal parts were used for storage and cooking. Water was kept in a skin bag. The lining of a buf-falo's stomach was used for cooking. Suspended from four sticks, it was filled with water. Hot stones were added until the water boiled. Meat or vegetables would be cooked in the water.

After a buffalo hunt, there was plenty of fresh meat to eat. The Sioux ate dried meat during the winter. Sometimes the men would hunt bear, deer, or antelope. Wild turkey and hens were eaten too. Women gathered wild fruits, cherries, berries, and plums. They also dug up vegetables, such as potatoes and prairie turnips. Food was shared by all, so no Sioux went hungry except during a famine.

When the announcement came that it was time to move, an entire village could be packed and ready to go in about fifteen minutes. Each family had a more or less permanent marching position in the procession. Three or four scouts led the group. The police or tykola (to ka la) kept the people in order. Penalties were severe for disobeying. Lingering behind or straying off to hunt was not allowed.

The Introduction of the Horse

A great influence on the lifestyle of the Plains Sioux was the introduction of the horse. No horses were found in North America when the Europeans first arrived. Spanish horses are thought to be the ancestors of American wild horses.

The Indians did not know about horses until 1519 when the Spanish brought them to America. Realizing how valuable horses were, the Spanish tried to keep the native people from learning to ride and manage horses. Eventually some horses were stolen. Soon all the Indians of the Plains acquired horses through trading or stealing. The Sioux obtained horses about 1742. In the 1800s, several million wild horses roamed parts of the American West.

The horse was a valuable addition to Sioux life. Here was an animal that could do the work of the dogs and also carry a rider. His size and strength enabled him to carry larger burdens and bigger travois. With the horse many more miles could be traveled during a move. To the Sioux this was a truly wondrous beast. They called it the "sacred dog."

The horse became a status symbol and was used for bartering. A family with many horses was considered wealthy. Since generosity was valued by the Sioux, it was a prime virtue to give horses away to the needy.

The Buffalo Economy

The buffalo hunters soon found the horse invaluable. Mounted on horseback, men could control much larger areas of land. The buffalo could be surrounded and killed with greater ease. On foot, a man could easily be gored or trampled, but a man on a trained horse could outrun a buffalo. He could ride alongside and shoot an arrow at point-blank range. Because the buffalo ran so fast, the hunters only had time to shoot about three arrows. The entire hunt was over in around ten minutes.

Boys were not allowed to ride with the hunters because of the danger involved. They often rode colts far behind and tried to shoot bows and arrows at the young buffalo calves that followed the herd. By the time a boy was ten, he was expected to have killed a calf.

With the horse, the Sioux economy flourished because of the constant supply of buffalo. After the men did the killing, the women were expected to do most of the work in preparing the meat and hides.

Buffalo meat was cut in thin strips and hung on frames to dry. After a few days it became hard. It was called jerky and could be eaten plain or boiled. When it was pounded into a powder, it was called pemmican. This could be kept in a storage box for years. Juneberries and chokeberries were often added to the pemmican to improve the taste.

Hides were prepared in two ways. One way made hard leather, called rawhide. Rawhide had many uses. It could be used for making moccasin soles, drums, rattles, and parfleches. Parfleches were

various-sized boxes and pouches used to carry small utensils, personal items, and dried meat. The other way of preparing the hide was to tan it. After the meat was scraped off, the hide was rubbed with a special tanning mixture of cooked brains and liver. It was then washed and rubbed with a sandstone. This made the leather nearly as soft as cloth. It could be used for moccasins, clothing, and tipis.

Both Sioux men and women were artistic and had an eye for beauty. The women made beautiful and elaborate ceremonial clothing. Everyday objects, such as a baby's cradleboard and storage boxes, were decorated. Porcupine quills colored with natural vegetable dyes were used to make intricate patterns. Later, glass beads were introduced by the white man. Beadwork became a highly developed craft.

Men used their artistic skills to paint pictures of their warring and hunting exploits on their tipis. The Sioux had no written language and kept a record of their past in pictures. This record was called the "winter count" because the Sioux counted the years by winters. Usually an old respected man was chosen to paint pictures of important events on deerskin. At the nighttime campfire, old men would use the pictures to remember these stories. In this way, tribal lore and tradition was passed on from generation to generation.

Buffalo horns were made into cups and spoons. Bowstrings and sewing equipment were made from sinew, which is the muscle along the buffalo's backbone. Buffalo hair was used for making ropes and decorations for belts. The Indians used every part of the carcass, never killing more buffalo than they needed.

Sioux Society

The Sioux society consisted of close-knit family hunting groups known as the "tiyospe." Individuals banded together under a common leader. Most often, they were related through descent or marriage. Under the guidance of their experienced elder leader, the group worked together in hunting and in war, in the daily chores of homemaking, and in rearing the children and caring for the aged. They also celebrated and worshiped together. They were a clannish group with loyalties directed toward the leader.

A child was a member of both of his parents' families. Boys generally associated themselves with their father's family, and girls connected with their mother's family. The birth of a child was a grand occasion. Within four days of the birth, a feast was held to name the baby. Infants were usually named after their oldest living grandparents, although sometimes the name of a highly respected deceased grandparent was used. Children had a second set of parents to help care for them. These people might be the baby's grandparents or they might be friends. Often the person was chosen because of a special skill which could be taught to the child.

Children learned different skills by helping their parents with all the work. Boys were taught how to become good hunters and warriors. They learned to make arrows and they learned how to shoot them. The most skilled boys were picked to ride with the scouts or run errands for the warriors. The women taught their daughters the skills they would need before getting married. Girls learned how to prepare animal skins, to make clothing, to cook, and to care for infants. Artistic skills, such as painting designs, quilling, and beadwork, were also encouraged. Girls practiced by making things for their families.

Until about 1750, marriages were often arranged by parents. Eventually this custom gave way to individual choice. If a couple had a common grandparent, they were not supposed to marry. A man was encouraged to choose a wife from outside his kinship group.

Usually a man tried to win honors in war and hunting before getting married. He made an effort to acquire many horses. Then he would go to the girl's tipi and play songs for her on his flute. If he thought the girl liked him, he would bring a horse to her family. When a couple agreed to marry, the young man would give her family more gifts and horses. Newlyweds usually lived near their parents. It was important for a new bride to keep up with her household chores. This ensured a successful marriage. If a man were rich enough, he sometimes had more than one wife. Often the wives were related to each other and shared the housekeeping burdens.

Marriage was an agreement of the moment. There were no vows spoken. If the marriage failed, it was the couples' affair and the family adjusted. Divorce was no great problem. A man simply announced that he had thrown away his woman. A woman could divorce her husband in a similar way. Membership in the family group changed through birth, death, and divorce, but an individual always had his family. He was responsible throughout his lifetime to these relatives regardless of his marital status.

A rare photograph of Sioux dancers, taken about 1890.

Medicine and Religion

The Sioux believed the Great Spirit, or Wakan Tanka (wahkahn tankah), had power over all things. Everything, including animals, trees, stones, and clouds, had a spirit or soul. The earth was the mother of all the spirits. The sun had great power because it gave light and warmth. The Sioux worshiped the spirits every day. The way they set their tipis, the way they ate and smoked their pipes, and the way they painted their faces was intended to please the spirits. Sometimes people prayed alone. Other times the whole tribe worshiped together and held a ceremony.

Visions in dreams were thought to come from the spirits. The medicine man, or shaman, was versed and trained in healing the sick and interpreting signs and dreams. He had a special understanding of the universe and knew the legendary traditions and beliefs supporting the Sioux religion. The shaman performed the rituals and ceremonies. The shaman was called on to interpret a boy's vision or dream during a ritual at the beginning of his manhood. At this time the boy would seek the spirit that would protect him the rest of his life. He was the people's wise and faithful spiritual counselor.

A rounded house called a sweat lodge was built with willow rods and then covered with skins. Inside the building, stones were heated in a fire pit and then water was poured over them to produce steam. The participant prayed as the hot steam purified his body. Sweat lodges were also used by warriors before a battle and by hunters before a big hunt.

The young man stayed in the sweat lodge for the required amount of time and then jumped into cold water. Next he was taken to a remote place and left alone without food or water, wearing only his breechcloth and moccasins. The next three or four days were spent praying for a special vision. At the end of

this time, men from the tribe came to help the young man back to the camp. After cleaning up and eating, he was taken to the shaman who would interpret his vision.

A young man might dream of a bird, animal, human spirit or an inanimate object. Sometimes his adult name was taken directly from his vision. Charms were fashioned for protection from the object of his vision. For example, if he dreamed of a bear, he might wear bearskin or carry a bear tooth to guard his against misfortune. When the shaman finished his interpretation, there would be a feast to celebrate his becoming a man.

A girl also went through a special ceremony to know her spirit. An old woman stayed with a girl for four days. During this time the girl prayed and did her chores. After the four days, the women took her to the shaman so he could interpret her dreams. Then the women bathed and dressed her in fine new clothes. A feast was held in her honor. The people sang and danced to celebrate her initiation into womanhood.

Curing the sick and wounded was the job of the shaman. Shamans had specialties. If one could not cure a particular problem, he would recommend another shaman. The Sioux believed sickness was the result of evil spirits or foreign substances entering the body. The shaman would determine the cause of the illness and then attempt to remove it. Sometimes a purifying bath was advised. Incense, chants with drums and rattles, and herbal medicines were used. Indians did not blame the shaman if a sick person did not get well. Maybe the sick person had not followed the instructions.

Generally, the Sioux were very healthy until the white man came. White man's diseases — especially scarlet fever, smallpox, and tuberculosis — killed more Indians than bullets did.

The Sun Dance was the most important ceremony of the year. This great celebration and feast was a time for the entire nation to assemble. It was held before the big buffalo hunt and lasted many days.

The men who danced inflicted pain upon themselves in return for special favors from the Great Spirit. They might pray for a life spared in battle, a sick child restored to health, or perhaps the end of a famine. A tree was selected and painted to serve as the sacred pole. It was raised with great care at the ceremonial place. The Sioux believed if it fell to the ground, they would suffer the worst bad luck.

On the fourth day, the shamans went to a nearby hill to greet the rising sun and pray for wisdom and strength for the dancers. Then the dance would begin. Some dancers vowed to look at the sun continuously. Other pierced their chest with a skewer attached to a rope that was tied to the sacred pole. They would dance without food or water until the skewer ripped out. Friends and relatives would sing to encourage them. The leader announced the end of the dance. There was great rejoicing and thanks given to the dancers for their sacrifice.

By about 1850, the people were no longer able to meet as one tribe. Wars and migration to the Great Plains made it difficult to assemble. Celebrations continued but in smaller groups. Today the dance is still performed on some Sioux reservations.

17

LIBRARY
California School for the Deaf
Riverside

Leisure and Fun

Life on the Plains was difficult, but the Sioux still had time for fun. Adults and children enjoyed a variety of activities for amusement. Many of the children's games centered around learning skills that would prepare them for adulthood. The Sioux loved to gamble, and few adult games were played without a wager.

There were races on foot and on horseback. Boys had contests in running, jumping and shooting arrows. Games were very rough, as this was a training ground on the path to becoming a warrior. Sometimes a boy was hurt badly, but this was expected and seldom was anyone angry over it. Guessing games were fun for everyone. The Moccasin Game involved three moccasins with a small pebble under one. Someone tried to guess where the pebble was. Adults played this game with bets. During the summer, boys and girls spent much time in the water and became expert swimmers.

If the autumn hunt had been successful, the people could relax in semi-permanent villages for the winter. They usually settled along wooded rivers. Moving camp and organizing large hunting expeditions were impractical in the cold season. Outdoor winter activities included sledding on bowed buffalo ribs, ice sliding, and spinning tops on the ice. Long, cold winter nights were perfect for storytelling. It was a good time for the old people to tell the next generation the tales and myths of the tribe.

(Photo courtesy of W.H. Over State Museum)

A mother and child relax on a travois hitched to a horse.

A Society Geared Toward War

The Sioux economy in the 1800s depended on the buffalo and the horse. The Sioux way was to dominate other tribes and capture their horses. This assured them control of the valuable buffalo country. The role of men was directed toward warfare. Prestige and wealth could be obtained through war. Warriors were the heroes.

Young boys were taught to handle bows and arrows. They played rough war games. By the time a boy was an adolescent, he was prepared to be a brave and enthusiastic warrior. War was the path to power and wealth. Many a warrior became a chief by distinguishing himself in battle. The Sioux ideal was to court danger and tempt death. Bravery was a foremost virtue for both men and women.

The bravest deed of all was to be the first to touch an enemy, dead or alive. A man kept count of his brave deeds by counting coup (koo). *Coup* is French for strike or blow. Another brave act was to sneak into an enemy camp and steal a horse. Hunters and warriors were respected according to the number of times they had accomplished brave deeds. A man was expected to brag about his coups.

War was thought of as a wonderful game. Most of the Sioux wars were not dangerous. The main object was to capture horses from enemy tribes and to win honors. The people accepted war as their way of life. The Sioux nation greedily guarded their wealth. By 1830, war was ingrained into their whole pattern of life. Their territory was vast, stretching from the Platte River to Canada and from Minnesota to Yellowstone. They also controlled the west bank of the Mississippi River.

The struggle between the British and the French and the American Revolution had little effect on the Sioux. To them, these were white man's wars far across the continent. By 1840 this feeling changed as the white man pushed into Sioux territory. The wonderful game of war became a death battle to save the Sioux way of life. The white man was coming to stay, and he was willing to kill to take over Indian land.

19

The Minnesota Uprising

The white man had many reasons for moving west. Missionaries, fur traders, government agents, and soldiers all came to live and work with the Indians. Originally there was no intent to take land away from the Indians. Traders relied on Indians for animal pelts, maple sugar, and wild rice. Indians wanted guns, kettles, blankets, and other goods. Both sides benefited from trading.

Fort Snelling was built in 1819 at the junction of the Mississippi and Minnesota rivers. American soldiers and government agents arrived at the fort to keep British fur traders out of American territory and to keep white settlers off Indian lands. Some agents felt the Indians should learn white man's ways. Missionaries came to convert the Indians to Christianity.

The Sioux still living in Minnesota were pressured to sell their land and

move to reservations. In 1837, they gave
in to these pressures and sold their land
east of the Mississippi River. The rest of
their land in Minnesota was sold to the
United States government in 1851. A
small reservation was set aside for them
in Minnesota. Payment to the Indians
was to be partly in cash, the rest in food,
seeds, and tools.

The idea was to turn the Minnesota
Sioux into farmers and Christians. The
Sioux traditional life was ignored and
they were told their ways were backward
and wrong. The white man's ways were
right. Some Sioux Indians accepted this
and tried to become farmers. Others
rebelled and wanted to save the old traditions. The people wanted to worship in
their own way. They missed the freedom
of the old days and did not like depend-
ing on the agency for food.

Tension between the white man and
the Sioux increased as the winter of 1862
set in. Food and supplies did not arrive
on schedule. The Sioux were hungry.

White traders would not give them supplies on credit. Some angry Sioux attacked white settlements, killing settlers
and taking others as hostages. The United States Army quickly retaliated with a
show of strength. By the end of six
weeks, about six hundred settlers and
soldiers and an unknown number of
Sioux Indians were dead. This event was
known as the Minnesota Uprising.

The United States government confis-
cated all lands assigned to the Eastern
Sioux. Thirty-eight Indians were put to
death for their part in the war. Other
Sioux escaped from Minnesota and fled
to the Dakotas, where they joined Sioux
tribes who had migrated 100 years ear-
lier. Some went to Canada. The Sioux
who remained in Minnesota were re-
moved to reservations in the Dakotas.
Sioux Indians everywhere were alarmed
and upset over the Minnesota Uprising.
The stage was set for more clashes between the white man and the Sioux
Indians.

Chief Red Cloud's Victory

(Photo courtesy of Smithsonian Institution)

Chief Red Cloud.

After the Minnesota Uprising the Sioux were angry and attacked wagon trains traveling west. Stagecoaches and telegraph lines were destroyed. White people were horrified as whole families were murdered. The Army responded by killing many Sioux in several North Dakota battles.

In 1865 a bill was passed in Congress authorizing new routes to the west through the great Teton buffalo ranges. This further enraged the Sioux. A warrior named Red Cloud emerged as a spokesman for the Sioux. He was a powerful leader and protested the building of new roads and military posts. His protests were ignored, but Red Cloud was determined to keep the white man out of Indian hunting lands. Forces were organized under Red Cloud, and for two years they harrassed the white people relentlessly.

With such effective resistance, the United States government was forced to negotiate. In 1868 the Fort Laramie Treaty was signed. The Great Sioux Reservation was established. It was to include all of what is now South Dakota west of the Missouri River. The United States agreed to keep whites off Indian lands and to abandon the proposed trail west. The Sioux agreed to release lands east of the Missouri with the exception of three reservations previously created. The Indians were to be paid for this land. Red Cloud refused to sign the treaty until he had seen the forts burn to the ground and the troops depart.

With this victory complete, Red Cloud agreed to lay down his arms. Promising to live peacefully, he took no part in further hostilities in the 1870s. His acceptance of reservation life caused tension with the other Indians who continued to fight the whites. The remainder of his life was spent trying to improve conditions for his people.

Chief Red Cloud made many trips to Washington, D.C. as a spokesman for the Sioux. His views were published in American newspapers, and he became well known for his excellent diplomacy. For thirty-nine years, Chief Red Cloud worked peacefully for his people. He made his last trip to Washington in 1897 when he was seventy-five years old. In 1909 Chief Red Cloud died at the age of eighty-seven in his Pine Ridge, South Dakota home.

Crazy Horse and the Battle of the Rosebud

Crazy Horse was a young man when he earned his reputation as a military genius among the Sioux. He did not want to settle on a reservation like Red Cloud. Staying out in the unceded buffalo country to the west, he had no intention of yielding to the white man. He was skilled in the techniques of Indian warfare as well as being courageous and daring.

In December, 1875, Crazy Horse and his people were far out on the plains in search of game. An order came from Washington for the Indians to come onto the reservations by the end of January, 1876. The message arrived too late for Crazy Horse to move his winter camp. The Indians were declared hostile and attacked by General George Crook. Escaping to the hills, Crazy Horse got his revenge the following spring.

Crazy Horse made his way to Sitting Bull's camp on the Rosebud River in the Valley of the Little Big Horn. Around three thousand warriors gathered. In June, 1876, Crazy Horse led a huge war party against the United States Army in the Battle of the Rosebud. General Crook was forced to withdraw with heavy losses of his troops.

Photo: © Korczak, Sc. Photo courtesy of Crazy Horse Memorial archives.

A statue of Crazy Horse, still emerging from the Black Hills of South Dakota. When completed, it will measure 563' high and 641' long, making it the largest sculpture in the world.

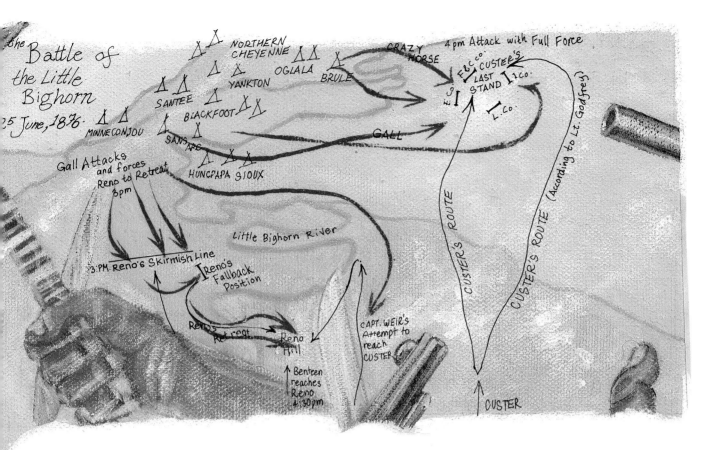

The Battle of the Little Bighorn
25 June, 1876.

NORTHERN CHEYENNE
OGLALA
BRULE
CRAZY HORSE
4pm Attack with Full Force
SANTEE
YANKTON
F&C CO. CUSTER'S LAST STAND
E CO.
L CO.
BLACKFOOT
MINNECONJOU
SANS ARC
GALL
HUNCPAPA SIOUX
Gall Attacks and forces Reno to Retreat 3pm
CUSTER'S ROUTE
CUSTER'S ROUTE (According to Lt. Godfrey)
Little Bighorn River
3:PM Reno's Skirmish Line
Reno's Fallback Position
Reno's Retreat
Reno Hill
CAPT. WEIR'S Attempt to reach CUSTER
Benteen reaches Reno 4:30pm
CUSTER

Custer's Last Stand

The U.S. Army faced powerful opponents in Crazy Horse and Sitting Bull. Sitting Bull was a medicine man with great influence and excellent abilities at planning and organization. He believed he had been divinely chosen to lead and protect his people. In June, 1876, he performed the Sun Dance and allowed himself to be tortured to gain a vision of what lay ahead for his people. He chanted prayers for his warriors. Sitting Bull had a dream that the Indians would defeat the whites in a great battle.

Fifteen thousand Plains Indians were gathered in a great camp along the Rosebud River. Chief Sitting Bull was chosen as supreme commander for the Sioux as well as the Cheyenne, the Arapaho, and the Blackfoot. After the Battle of the Rosebud, the people felt they had won a great victory. The tribes were restless and wanted to leave the large camp. Sitting Bull felt the greater battle was yet to come and encouraged the people to stay together.

Meanwhile, General George Custer moved into the valley of the Little Big Horn and sighted the Indian campfires. General Custer had achieved great fame as an Indian fighter. Many of his rivals felt Custer needlessly risked the lives of his men. General Custer had been ordered to wait for more soldiers but he was anxious for fame and glory. Greatly underestimating Indian strength, he attacked the camp. The battle, known as Custer's Last Stand, was brief. Every soldier was killed within two hours. It was a great victory for the Indians, but it was their last.

The Defeat of the Sioux

After their triumph over Custer, the Indians scattered into smaller camps to hunt buffalo. U.S. Army forces constantly pursued and attacked the smaller groups of Indians. After Custer's Last Stand, soldiers were out for revenge and killed old people, children, and women. As more and more soldiers poured in their country, one after another of the Sioux chiefs were forced to surrender. Chief Sitting Bull fled to Canada. Chief Crazy Horse stayed behind.

The buffalo were disappearing as white commercial hunters slaughtered the herds. Eventually the food supply became inadequate. Crazy Horse was lured out of hiding. After surrendering to his old adversary General Crook, Chief Crazy Horse found he had been tricked. He flew into a rage and drew his knife. A white soldier stabbed Crazy Horse in the back and killed him.

Because the Canadian government refused to give Sitting Bull a reservation, he returned to the United States in 1881. Chief Sitting Bull was allowed to live on a reservation at Standing Rock, South Dakota (part of this reservation is in North Dakota).

In the years that followed, the Indian lands became smaller and smaller. The Black Hills, which the Sioux considered sacred lands, were seized by the United States. By 1889 the Great Sioux Reservation was broken up into smaller reservations, making nine million acres available for white settlers.

During the 1890s, the Sioux were frustrated by their confinement in the reservations. They turned to a supernatural cult called the Ghost Dance. A Paiute Indian claimed he was a prophet and had received a message from the Great Spirit. He said that if the Indians danced the Ghost Dance, their old life would be restored to them. Buffalo would return, dead Indians would come back to earth and the white man would disappear. The Ghost Dance spread quickly throughout the reservations.

Sitting Bull did not believe the prophecies but he saw no harm in allowing his people to dance. Many white people became frightened that the Ghost Dance would cause further uprising and hostilities. One Indian agent became suspicious of Sitting Bull and ordered his arrest. Unwilling to leave his home, a tragic fight occurred on December 13, 1890. Chief Sitting Bull, his seventeen-year-old son, Crowfoot, and six other members of his tribe were killed.

The final defeat of the Sioux Indians came two weeks later on December 29, 1890. After Chief Sitting Bull was killed, the army ordered all Sioux to surrender their weapons. One group fled, hoping to join Chief Red Cloud at Pine Ridge. On their journey the tribe camped at Wounded Knee Creek. They were hunted down and surrounded by army troops. Not surrendering quickly enough, the troops opened fire, killing over 100 men, women, and children. It was called the Battle of Wounded Knee, but it was really a massacre. This tragedy ended Sioux resistance to the white man once and for all.

A mass burial follows the Battle of Wounded Knee.

(Photo courtesy of Nebraska State Historical Society)

(Photo by Bill Noll, courtesy of Little Wound School)

Left: Poet Ray Young Bear reviews a poem by a student.

Below: Teacher Misty Brave helps Alberta White Face with a science project.

(Photo by Bill Noll, courtesy of Little Wound School)

Sioux Today

Life in the twentieth century has been difficult for the Sioux Indians, as it has been for all Native Americans. For a long time the Indians were not allowed to govern themselves. The U.S. Bureau of Indian Affairs managed all their affairs. Indian children were often taken from their parents and sent to boarding schools. Children were punished for using Indian languages and practicing traditional ways. The Sioux were forced to learn the white man's religion, language, and way of life.

Some Indians were able to make the transition to living like a white man. Others resisted and are still resisting today. Indians want a good standard of living. They do not believe that they must give up all their traditions and live exactly like a white person. American history texts and movies have often portrayed the Indian as savage and primitive. Many white people still have this attitude toward Indians, but it is slowly changing.

Today the great Siouan group of tribes are scattered throughout the United States. About thirty thousand Sioux live on nine reservations in South Dakota. There are also smaller reservations in North Dakota, Nebraska, and northeastern Montana. A few Sioux live in Canada and others in small towns in the Great Lakes states.

The white pioneers settled on the best lands, and the U.S. government took what they wanted for dam sites. Reservation lands are poor, and few crops can be grown. Poverty became a way of life for many Indians. Some Sioux migrated to cities to find work in businesses and factories. Very often they were the last to be hired and the first to be fired.

Unfair treatment by the U.S. government has caused trouble between Indian activists and white political leaders. For example, the U.S. government seized 500 square miles of the Sioux Pine Ridge Reservation to use as a practice bombing range in 1942. Broken treaties, poverty, bad housing, and poor schooling are other Indian complaints. Frustrated Indians have stages a series of demonstrations to dramatize their problems. In 1973, one group took over the town of Wounded Knee at gunpoint to demonstrate for the rights of Indians. Many Indians were brought to trial for this action. The federal judge dismissed all charges due to evidence of misconduct on the part of United States agents.

Sioux tribes today are usually governed by a tribal council with a chair-man and other officers elected at large by the tribe. The leaders are exploring every means of improving tribal economies. Natural resources such as sand, gravel, and some oil and coal are being developed. Small industries have been established. Plants that employ Indians make a variety of items from cheese to automobile mufflers.

Education is encouraged, with programs for adults as well as Head Start programs for preschoolers. An earn-and-learn program helps high schoolers. Unemployed, unskilled adults are assisted with work experience programs. More students are going on for higher education, often with the help of scholarships.

Today the Sioux strive to preserve their traditional ways and yet improve their standard of living. They need compassion and understanding as they move forward toward a life of peace and harmony, a life that links the old with the new.

(Photo by Bill Noll, courtesy of Little Wound School)

Misty Brave and her sixth grade students work on a computer at Little Wound School, Kyle, South Dakota.

Important Dates in Sioux History

1500s	A Siouan group of tribes migrate westward from eastern and midwestern United States. Some settle in Minnesota as woodland Indians.
1519	Horses are brought to America by the Spanish.
1700s	The Sioux begin a migration to the Great Plains.
1740s	The Sioux obtain horses and learn to use them effectively.
1750	The Sioux are firmly established as nomadic buffalo hunters. For the next 100 years, they dominate other tribes on the Great Plains and guard their territory.
1819	Fort Snelling is built at the junction of the Mississippi and Minnesota rivers for American soldiers and government agents.
1851	The Eastern Sioux are pressured to sell land in Minnesota and move to reservations.
1862	Hungry, discouraged Eastern Sioux rebel in the Minnesota Uprising.
1865	Congress passes a bill authorizing new routes to the west through the great Teton buffalo ranges.
1868	Fort Laramie Treaty is signed, also known as Chief Red Cloud's victory. Great Sioux Reservation is established.
1875	In December, an order from Washington requires Indians to report to reservations by end of January, 1876, or be declared hostile.
1876	Crazy Horse's winter camp is attacked by General Crook; the Indians flee to the hills. In early June, Sitting Bull dances Sun Dance and has vision of victory for his people. In late June, General Crook is defeated at Battle of the Rosebud. General Custer is defeated at Battle of Little Big Horn.
1877	Crazy Horse is killed in a misunderstanding; the U.S. takes over the Black Hills.
1880s	The Great Sioux Reservation is broken into smaller reservations.
1890s	The Sioux dance the Ghost Dance.
1890	Sitting Bull is arrested and killed in tragic fight on December 13.
1890	The Battle of Wounded Knee on December 29 ends Sioux resistance.
1924	The U.S. recognizes all Indians as citizens of the U.S.
1934	The Indian Reorganization Act provides money for Indian development.
1942	The U.S. government seizes 500 square miles of Sioux reservation to use as a practice bombing range.
1944	The National Congress of American Indians is formed to lobby in Washington for Indian rights and benefits.
1973	A Sioux activist group holds protest at Wounded Knee.
1982	Sioux lose fight in Supreme Court to regain ownership of the Black Hills of South Dakota.

INDEX